Pocket Books

W9-BYQ-650

Cats

Kane Miller
A DIVISION OF EDC PUBLISHING

First American Edition 2019
Kane Miller, A Division of EDC Publishing

For information contact:
Kane Miller, A Division of EDC Publishing
5402 S 122nd E Ave
Tulsa, OK 74146
www.kanemiller.com

Printed and bound in China, December 2022
ISBN: 978-1-61067-877-3 Library of Congress Control Number: 2018942403

Images © Frank Lane Picture Agency: german rex, sokoke, pixie bob © J.-L. Klein and M.-L. Hubert/FLPA
laperm © Sabine Schwerdtfeger/Tierfotoagentur/FLPA. Images © Animal-Photography.com: oriental
longhair, seychellois, smoke asian, tabby asian, tiffanie © Alan Robinson, american wirehair, australian mist,
highlander, Javanese, kinkalow, kurilian bobtail longhair, lambkin, napoleon, pixie bob © Helmi Flick,
brazilian shorthair, ojos azules © Tetsu Yamazaki. Images © Dreamstime.com: Aegean © Michal Bednarek,
american curl © Csaba Vanyi, british shorthair © Miraswonderland, british shorthair colorpoint © Nicksu |,
burmilla © Vanessa Tay, burmilla, Burmese © Yelizaveta Tomashevska, chausie © Taniawild, Himalayan ©
John Wollwerth, japanese bobtail © Vagengeym, laperm longhair © Linncurrie, munchkin © Nisara
Sriployrung, munchkin, peterbald © Ires007, serengeti © Kucher Serhii, siamese, foldex, lykoi © Isselee,
somali © Nelikz, sphinx © Pavlo Vakhrushev, sphynx, persian bicolor © Dmitri Pravdjukov, york chocolate ©
Anna Krivitskaia. Images © Shutterstock.com: li hua © FrimuFilms, Abyssinian © nelik, american bobtail ©
Konovalov Yevhenii, american bobtail longhair © Seregraff, american bobtail shorthair © OrangeGroup,
american Burmese © otsphoto, american curl © maxkrapiva, american shorthair © Paisit Teeraphatsakool,
american shorthair © Vladyslav Starozhylov, american shorthair (face) © urska petek, australian mist ©
Daniel Thompson, balinese © Rika-sama, bambino, persian chinchilla, persian smoke, siamese - tabby-
pointed, turkish van © Linn Currie, bengal © Anastasiia Chystokoliana, bengal © Seregraff, birman,
chartreux, devon rex, european shorthair, exotic shorthair, oriental foreign white, persian self, selkirk rex ©
Eric Isselee, bombay © Viktor Sergeevich, british longhair, savannah © kuban_girl, toybob © Seregraff,
british shorthair black and white cat © alexavo, british shorthair tortie, oriental tortie, singapura © Krissi
Lundgren, cat sleeping © Vika Hova, cat's claw © Pavel Shlykov, chantilly-tiffany © Lukas Beno, cornish rex ©
Okssi, cymric © garmoncheg, dwelf, oriental bicolor © Jenni Ferreira, egyptian mau © ARTSILENSE, ginger
cat lying in bed © Konstantin Aksenov, havanna, oriental self © Bildagentur Zoonar GmbH, highland ©
SUSAN LEGGETT, khao manee © Peefay, kittens fighting © Tony Campbell, korat © Gino Santa Maria, maine
coon cat © Svetography, manx © NSC Photography, nebelung © Angel72, neva masquerade © Zharinova
Marina, norwegian forest cat © Elisa Putti, oriental shaded © Ed Phillips, oriental smoke © Anna Jurkovska,
oriental tabby © mdmmikle, ragamuffin © Scampi, ragdoll © Atmosphere1, russian blue © Kirill Vorobyev,
scottish fold shorthair, aphrodite giant, scottish fold longhair © alexavol, selkirk rex shorthair © Jagodka,
siberian © Pavel Sepi, skookum © Robynrg, snowshoe © nevodka, sphinx © Elya Vatel, thai, ocicat, japanese
bobtail shorthair, kurilean bobtail shorthair © dien, tiger © Vladimir Wrangel, tonkinese © dezy, toyger ©
Ivanova N, turkish angora © MirasWonderland, turkish angora © StockPhotosArt, white british shorthair ©
Grigorita Ko, siamese tortie point © Glass and Nature. Images © Istock.com: arabian mau © Jolkesky,
california spangled © meanmachine77.

Introducing cats

Cats belong to the family of mammals called Felidae that contains over 35 species, from "big cats" like tigers to domestic "small cats." Catlike carnivores first appeared tens of millions of years ago, but their close relationship with humans only started about 4,000–7,000 years ago. Cats that were used to protect food stores from rodents became status symbols and then treasured companions and pets.

Domestic cats are related to larger cats such as this Siberian tiger.

Retractable claws slide back into sheaths for stealthy movement.

Through play, kittens develop the skills needed to hunt.

Characteristics of cats

Cats' bodies are built for hunting. Even a house cat is a skilled predator. It has sharp senses to detect prey, an athletic body to chase it down, and claws and teeth to catch and kill.

Cats' eyes are forward facing for judging distances when hunting. Powerful legs propel them when running, pouncing and jumping. Their tails have a wide range of movements to aid balance.

Adult cats have 30 teeth for gripping, cutting and grooming. Their retractable curved claws are used to scratch, fight and grip.

How to use this book

This book gives you the essential facts and information on 118 fabulous, furry (or hairless!) felines.

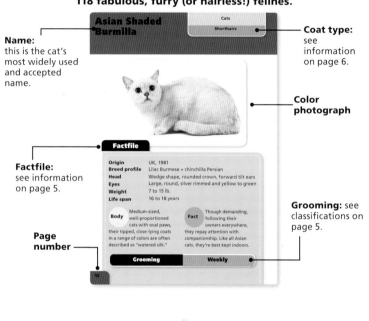

Name: this is the cat's most widely used and accepted name.

Asian Shaded Burmilla

Cats
Shorthairs

Coat type: see information on page 6.

Color photograph

Factfile: see information on page 5.

Factfile

Origin	UK, 1981
Breed profile	Lilac Burmese + chinchilla Persian
Head	Wedge shape, rounded crown, forward tilt ears
Eyes	Large, round, silver rimmed and yellow to green
Weight	7 to 15 lb.
Life span	16 to 18 years

Body Medium-sized, well-proportioned cats with oval paws, their tipped, close-lying coats in a range of colors are often described as "watered silk."

Fact Though demanding, following their owners everywhere, they repay attention with companionship. Like all Asian cats, they're best kept indoors.

Grooming: see classifications on page 5.

Page number

Grooming | Weekly

12

A British shorthair on the prowl.

Factfile

The Factfiles provide key facts and figures about each cat, including its origin, appearance and weight.

Origin
The year (if available) and place first formally bred or recognized.

Breed profile
The breeds used to develop a new type or breed of cat.

Head
Significant features, including shape and size.

Eyes
Eye size, shape, spacing or angle; eye color or other features of significance.

Weight
The weight range of an adult cat: lower figure shows minimum female weight; higher figure shows maximum male weight.

Life span
Average life of the breed.

Body Learn about the breed's build and shape, unique features, coat colors and patterns.

Fact Discover more about the breed's history, personality, abilities, likes and dislikes.

Grooming

Each breed has been given a grooming classification, indicating the frequency of combing and bathing required to maintain a healthy coat. Grooming also helps a cat bond with its owner.

Weekly	2 to 3 times a week	Daily
Brushing once a week helps distribute natural oils necessary to maintain healthy skin and coat.	Frequent brushing addresses tangles before they turn into mats, and allows for checking for any skin or ear problems.	A few minutes of grooming every day maintains longhaired breeds' coats and keeps them healthy.

Coat type

The breeds in this book are separated into shorthair and longhair cats. Shorthair and longhair cats belonging to the same breed are usually identical in every way except for the length of their coats.

Shorthair cats

Most Felidae – wild and domestic – evolved with short hair so they could run through grasslands and dense forests without catching their fur. Hairless cats are included in this group because they actually have a coat of very fine hair.

A shorthair cat requires less grooming than a longhair, while hairless cats need regular wiping or bathing. A benefit of short hair is that any parasites or injuries on a cat's body are easier to spot and treat.

A shorthaired Bengal is perfectly acclimated for warm climates.

Longhair cats

It is believed that long hair is the result of a genetic mutation that increased the breed's chance of survival in cold climates, though some longhairs resulted from breeding programs that aimed to introduce the genes for long hair into shorthair breeds.

Cats shed their coats in spring. Some longhairs look very different after shedding!

A Maine coon's coat helps keep it warm in cold weather.

Feline facts

Cats in ancient Egypt were so highly regarded that they were often ceremonially mummified when they died.

A cat's tongue feels rough because the upper surface is covered in small, hornlike structures called *filiform papillae*. These are an aid to grooming, help rip meat from bones, and are used to lap up liquids.

A cat's whiskers are used as touch receptors. They are embedded deeper into the cat's skin than the fur of its coat.

Whiskers are connected to the cat's muscular and nervous systems and send information about the cat's surroundings directly to its sensory nerves.

Cats spend about 65 days in the womb. Newborn kittens usually measure from 4 to 6 inches long, and weigh between 2 and 5 ounces. The average size of a cat's litter is four, but in 1970 one cat gave birth to no less than 19 kittens!

A cat's night vision enables it to see six times better than a human.

Contents

Shorthair cats	**8**
Longhair cats	**88**
Glossary	126
Index	128

Cats usually live about 9 to 15 years, although it is not uncommon for some cats to reach the age of 20 or more.

It is believed that cats can make about 17 different sounds. The main types are meows, hisses, purrs and chirps.

Cats tend to sleep around 16 hours a day. While asleep, their brain remains alert and their senses active.

Domestic cats are able to purr when they inhale and exhale, but they cannot roar. Big cats, such as lions and tigers, can "purr" only on an exhale, but are of course, better known for their loud roars!

Exotic Shorthair

Factfile

Origin	USA, 1960s
Breed profile	American shorthair + silver Persian
Head	Rounded shape, flat face, full cheeks, small ears
Eyes	Huge, round, wide set in a range of colors
Weight	7 to 12 lb.
Life span	8 to 15 years

Body The exotic shorthair has a short, rounded, stocky body, with soft fur and a thick undercoat. The coat can be almost any color and pattern. It does not shed.

Fact Known as the "lazy person's Persian" for its easier grooming needs, this loves-to-be-loved lap cat is one of the most popular breeds in the US.

Grooming Weekly

Khao Manee

Factfile

Origin	Thailand, 1300s
Breed profile	Naturally evolved
Head	Heart shape, high cheeks, large upright ears
Eyes	Rounded oval in any color or odd eyed
Weight	6 to 12 lb.
Life span	10 to 15 years

Body Khao manee (Thai for "white gem") have smooth white coats with short, close-lying fur and slender, athletic bodies. They are active and intelligent.

Fact Cats with one blue and one yellow eye are regarded as lucky, but two canary-yellow eyes are also popular and much desired.

Grooming	**Weekly**

Korat

Factfile

Origin	Thailand, 1100s to 1500s
Breed profile	Naturally evolved
Head	Heart shape with large, round-tipped ears
Eyes	Large, walnut shape, brilliant green (adult)
Weight	7 to 11 lb.
Life span	10 to 15 years

Body The shimmering silver-blue coat is created by hairs that are light colored at the root, darker in the middle and silvery at the tips. The spine curves upward.

Fact The first pure Korats were bred in the US in 1959. They were then crossed with self blue Siamese to avoid inbreeding, creating the US line.

Grooming	Weekly

Chinese Li Hua

Factfile

Origin	China, 1300 BCE
Breed profile	Naturally evolved Chinese mountain cat
Head	Large, diamond shape, ears are often tufted
Eyes	Almond shape, angled in green, yellow or brown
Weight	9 to 12 lb.
Life span	9 to 16 years (some estimates 15 to 20 years)

Body Large, muscly and robust cats, their thick, brown-mackerel tabby coats come from fur that is black at the roots, light-yellow in the middle and brown at the tips.

Fact First recognized as a breed in 2010, and also known as Dragon Li, their heritage makes them good hunters and – sometimes! – trainable pets.

Grooming	Weekly

Asian Shaded Burmilla

Factfile

Origin	UK, 1981
Breed profile	Lilac Burmese + chinchilla Persian
Head	Wedge shape, rounded crown, forward tilt ears
Eyes	Large, round, silver rimmed and yellow to green
Weight	7 to 15 lb.
Life span	16 to 18 years

Body Medium-sized, well-proportioned cats with oval paws, their tipped, close-lying coats in a range of colors are often described as "watered silk."

Fact Though demanding, following their owners everywhere, they repay attention with companionship. Like all Asian cats, they're best kept indoors.

Grooming	Weekly

Factfile

Origin	UK, 1981
Breed profile	Lilac Burmese + chinchilla Persian
Head	Wedge shape, rounded crown, forward tilt ears
Eyes	Large, round, silver rimmed and yellow to green
Weight	7 to 15 lb.
Life span	16 to 18 years

Body Asian smoke features match those of others in the Asian group, including a face structure that can cause breathing problems and loud snoring.

Fact The top coat is mostly solid colored (tabby markings are minimal); the undercoat, silver. With movement, the undercoat shows like wisps of smoke.

Grooming	Weekly

Factfile

Origin	UK, 1981
Breed profile	Lilac Burmese + chinchilla Persian
Head	Wedge shape, rounded crown, forward tilt ears
Eyes	Large, round, silver rimmed and yellow to green
Weight	7 to 15 lb.
Life span	16 to 18 years

Body The tail of Asian group cats is medium to long in length, and tapers evenly to the tip. If gently brought forward, the tail extends to the shoulder.

Fact The coat of the Asian tabby may be classic (blotched), spotted (stripes appear as spots), mackerel (vertical curved stripes) or ticked (colored bands on each hair).

Grooming	Weekly

Bombay

Factfile

Origin	USA, 1965
Breed profile	Sable Burmese + black American shorthair
Head	Broad and round with round-tipped ears
Eyes	Large almond shape, wide set, golden to copper
Weight	6 to 12 lb.
Life span	12 to 20 years (estimates vary widely)

Body Muscly and rounded, this medium-sized cat is black from the end of its snubbed nose and mouth to its paw pads and the tip of its straight tail.

Fact The Bombay is a very vocal cat, often compared to a black panther because of its sleek, glossy coat and the way its body sways as it walks.

Grooming	Weekly

15

Singapura

Factfile

Origin	USA or Singapore, 1975 (unconfirmed)
Breed profile	Naturally evolved (unconfirmed)
Head	Large and round, large ears, blunt muzzle
Eyes	Large, round and gray to yellow
Weight	4 to 8 lb.
Life span	9 to 15 years

Body One of the smallest cats, the singapura's stocky, muscly body has sepia-brown over cream fur, and may result from an Abyssinian-Burmese cross.

Fact A playful cat that loves human company, they seek out high resting and vantage points and will often ride on their owner's shoulders.

Grooming	Weekly

16

European Burmese

Factfile

Origin	UK, 1963
Breed profile	Blue American Burmese + red British shorthair
Head	Rounded crown, wide cheeks, forward tilt ears
Eyes	Large, angled to nose in yellow to amber
Weight	6 to 10 lb.
Life span	10 to 15 years

Body These Burmese have a gently rounded body on slender legs, small oval paws, and a fine, satin-like, close-lying coat with little or no undercoat.

Fact Crossing has yielded many colors for the breed including brown, blue, lilac, chocolate, red and cream. Also brown, chocolate, blue and lilac tortoiseshell.

Grooming	Weekly

American Burmese

Factfile

Origin	USA, 1936
Breed profile	Burmese–Siamese + American Siamese
Head	Wedge shape, full cheeks, large pointed ears
Eyes	Rounded almond, wide set in yellow to golden
Weight	8 to 14 lb.
Life span	10 to 15 years

Body Heavier than they look, with a close-lying coat, American Burmese are often described as "bricks wrapped in silk." These "bricks" love lap time.

Fact Wong Mau was the Burmese-Siamese (Tonkinese) cat at the start of the US breeding program. Some class the UK Burmese as a separate breed.

Grooming	Weekly

Factfile

Origin	Thailand and Myanmar, or USA, 1950s
Breed profile	Siamese + Burmese
Head	Rounded, wedge shape with wide-set ears
Eyes	Peach pit shape in green to light blue
Weight	6 to 12 lb.
Life span	10 to 15 years

Body Its muscular body is supported by slim legs and oval paws. The short coat is soft, silky and dense, and darker colored on the face, ears, legs and tail.

Fact Wong Mau was probably the first (see p.18), but no matter its lineage, today's Tonk is nosy, independent and comes in many color and pattern variations.

Grooming	Weekly

Oriental
Foreign White

Factfile

Origin	UK, 1962
Breed profile	Seal-point Siamese + white British shorthair
Head	Long wedge shape with large, pricked ears
Eyes	Almond shape, angled to nose and bright blue
Weight	5 to 12 lb.
Life span	12 to 15 years

Body
This lean, pure-white cat has a long neck, body and legs. The rump stands higher than the shoulders, with a whiplike tail. It always looks alert!

Fact
Hypoallergenic (almost), they are not mated together, in order to keep the breed's white coat and blue eyes, and to avoid deafness.

Grooming	Weekly

Oriental Self

Factfile

Origin	UK, 1950s
Breed profile	Siamese + Russian blue/Br. shorthair/Abyssinian
Head	Long wedge shape with large, pricked ears
Eyes	Almond shape, angled to nose, fleckless green
Weight	5 to 12 lb.
Life span	12 to 15 years

Body The long neck and limbs and fine bone structure are pure Siamese, but the brown, red, blue, cream, lilac and ebony coat colors set Orientals apart.

Fact Like all Orientals, this one likes sunbathing, but too much sun can cause the ears and tail – or the whole cat! – to change color.

Grooming	Weekly

Oriental Smoke

Factfile

Origin	UK, 1971
Breed profile	Red-point Siamese + shaded silver shorthair
Head	Long, wedge shape with large, pricked ears
Eyes	Almond shape, angled to nose, fleckless green
Weight	5 to 12 lb.
Life span	12 to 15 years

Body When viewed from the side, the nose of Orientals should be straight, with the tip in perfect vertical alignment with the tip of the chin.

Fact The bottom third or more of each coat hair is white, only seen when the coat is parted, with the top third or more solid colored.

Grooming	Weekly

Oriental Shaded

Factfile

Origin	UK, 1970s
Breed profile	Chocolate-point Siamese + Persian chinchilla
Head	Long wedge shape with large, pricked ears
Eyes	Almond shape, angled to nose, fleckless green
Weight	5 to 12 lb.
Life span	12 to 15 years

Body An adult may show faint tabby markings, but the ideal standard is for the undercoat to be a paler shade of the tip color.

Fact All the Oriental cats are intelligent and need stimulation and company. They are very "talkative," too, and prefer high perches.

Grooming	**Weekly**

Oriental Tabby

Factfile

Origin	UK, 1970s
Breed profile	Siamese + domestic shorthair tabby
Head	Long wedge shape with large, pricked ears
Eyes	Almond shape, angled to nose, fleckless green
Weight	5 to 12 lb.
Life span	12 to 15 years

Body There are 112 possible combinations of colors and patterns for this tabby, with faces having the signature "M" and the coat hairs banded.

Fact Oriental cats are robust, their tubular bodies pure muscle. They are lean, keen, raspy meowing attention seekers – owners ignore at their peril.

Grooming	Weekly

Oriental Tortie

Factfile

Origin	UK, 1960s
Breed profile	Red-point Siamese + Havana browns and blacks
Head	Long wedge shape with large, pricked ears
Eyes	Almond shape, angled to nose, fleckless green
Weight	5 to 12 lb.
Life span	12 to 15 years

Body This tortoiseshell's coat has closely mixed or evenly distributed patches of red-orange and cream over a black, brown or cinnamon coat.

Fact Two X chromosomes are needed for the tortoiseshell pattern to appear, so cats are usually female (males are very rare and often sterile).

Grooming	**Weekly**

Oriental Bicolor

Factfile

Origin	USA, 1979
Breed profile	Siamese + bicolor American shorthair
Head	Long wedge shape with large, pricked ears
Eyes	Almond shape, angled to nose, fleckless green
Weight	5 to 12 lb.
Life span	12 to 15 years

Body Oriental bicolors almost look as though they've been splashed with white paint. About a third of the solid coat (mostly legs and underside) is white.

Fact Oriental cats are among the most popular domestic cats in the world, and are a Cat Fanciers' Association (CFA) recognized pedigree.

Grooming	Weekly

Havana Brown

Factfile

Origin	UK, 1952 and USA, 1960s
Breed profile	Chocolate/seal-point Siamese + black shorthair
Head	Triangular with square muzzle, forward tilt ears
Eyes	Oval and vivid emerald green (preferred)
Weight	6 to 10 lb.
Life span	10 to 15 years

Body A reddish-brown coat covers a muscular body, with mature cats showing no markings. Whiskers are the same color as the coat, but pads are pink.

Fact Rare and endangered, it is estimated that there are only 1,000 Havanas in the world. US-bred Havana head shape is different than UK bred.

Grooming	Weekly

Factfile

Origin	Thailand, with redevelopment in the 1980s
Breed profile	Naturally evolved Thai Wichin-maat cat
Head	Wedge shaped, round cheeks, flat forehead
Eyes	Rounded and deep blue
Weight	6 to 12 lb.
Life span	12 to 15 years

Body
The Thai has a medium-sized build, with a dark (though not extreme) pointed coat that is short, loose and flat.

Fact
Thais share ancestry and point coloration with the Siamese but are a distinct breed; modern breeding aims to be true to the original native.

Grooming	Weekly

Siamese Self Pointed

Factfile

Origin	Thailand and later UK and USA development
Breed profile	Naturally evolved
Head	Long wedge shape with broad, wide-set ears
Eyes	Almond shape, angled to nose and bright blue
Weight	6 to 12 lb.
Life span	15 to 20 years

Body Siamese have long, tubular, muscular bodies and legs. The pale coat has darker points on face, tail, ears and feet, which appear one month after birth.

Fact Today's Siamese breeders accentuate the lean, long form and head shape. The original native cat was rounder, with a more apple-shaped head.

Grooming	**Weekly**

29

Factfile

Origin	UK, 1940s to 1960s
Breed profile	Seal-point Siamese + unknown cat
Head	Long wedge shape with broad wide-set ears
Eyes	Almond shape, angled to nose and bright blue
Weight	6 to 12 lb.
Life span	15 to 20 years

Body Displaying typical tabby patterns and "M" on the forehead, Siamese point colors include seal, blue, chocolate, lilac, red, cream, cinnamon and fawn.

Fact The first tabby point was the result of a seal point and unknown cross. It wasn't until years later that the type was recognized as Siamese.

Grooming	Weekly

Siamese Tortie Pointed

Factfile

Origin   UK, 1940s to 1960s
Breed profile   Siamese with orange gene + Siamese
Head shape   Long wedge shape with broad wide-set ears
Eyes   Almond shape, angled to nose and bright blue
Weight   6 to 12 lb.
Life span   15 to 20 years

Body Every tortie point has unique mottling on its points. The solid-color body coat determines mottling color. Body mottling may appear on older cats.

Fact Like all Siamese, the tortie point can be loud, vocalizing a wide variety of different sounds. Siamese are known for being chatty!

Grooming	Weekly

31

Factfile

Origin	UK, 1980s
Breed profile	Bicolor Persian + Siamese + Oriental
Head	Wedge shape with large, wide-spaced ears
Eyes	Almond shape and brilliant blue
Weight	9 to 14 lb.
Life span	12 to 15 years

Body These elegant cats have sleek, elongated bodies, long legs and large distinctive ears. Coats are white, with patches of color on points and body.

Fact Seychellois were bred to develop the coat patterns of a native Seychelles cat with Oriental limbs and head and Siamese build and personality.

Grooming	Weekly

Snowshoe

Factfile

Origin	USA, 1960s
Breed profile	White-pawed Siamese + tuxedo Am. shorthair
Head	Slightly rounded and wedge shaped
Eyes	Walnut shape and blue
Weight	7 to 12 lb.
Life span	14 to 19 years

Body Snowshoe bodies have shorthair bulk with Siamese length, coat colors and markings. Paws are white, and the face displays a distinctive inverted "V."

Fact Internet sensation Grumpy Cat has snowshoe markings, but her parentage is uncertain. Still, snowshoe cats are typically very chill.

Grooming	Weekly

American Shorthair

Factfile

Origin	USA, 1904
Breed profile	European domestic cat + British shorthair
Head	Broad and round with small, high-set ears
Eyes	Large and wide in five colors and odd eyed
Weight	6 to 15 lb.
Life span	15 to 20 years

Body This robust cat has a well-developed body with straight legs and strong jaw. Its short, thick coat comes in 80 types. The most popular is the silver tabby.

Fact This cat is descended from the Pilgrims' rat catchers in the 1600s. Later breeding retained these mousers' color and temperament.

Grooming	2 to 3 times a week

European Shorthair

Factfile

Origin	Sweden, 1980s
Breed profile	Non-pedigree European domestic cats
Head	Large, round face with well-developed cheeks
Eyes	Round and mostly blue, amber and green
Weight	8 to 15 lb.
Life span	15 to 20 years

Body This shorthair has a firm, rounded body and dense, shiny coat in many colors and patterns. It is an independent, smart and active outdoor cat.

Fact Finland's national cat, they are descended from working cats spread across Europe by the ancient Romans, and retain similar qualities.

Grooming	Weekly

Factfile

Origin	Brazil, 1500s
Breed profile	Brazilian feral street cats
Head	Longer than it is wide with large, pointed ears
Eyes	Large, round and in coat-related colors
Weight	8 to 16 lb.
Life span	14 to 20 years

Body The Brazilian is a large, strong cat with a mid-length tail that tapers to the tip. Its shape is elegant, and its silky coat comes in every color and pattern.

Fact This breed's 500-year-old ancestors arrived with the Portuguese. The cats that thrived created a distinct breed that was confirmed in 1998.

Grooming	Weekly

Chartreux

Factfile

Origin	France, 1500s (or earlier)
Breed profile	Feral Middle East mountain cats (unconfirmed)
Head	Round, broad, full cheeked with smiley expression
Eyes	Round, well spaced and yellow to orange
Weight	7 to 16 lb.
Life span	12 to 15 years

Body The chartreux's stocky body rests on short, skinny legs. It has a blue-gray nose, lightly tufted coat, blue lips and rose-brown pads.

Fact The national *chat* of France, a chartreux's pedigree name relates to its birth year. Chartreux born in 2018 have names that start with "O."

Grooming — **2 to 3 times a week**

Russian Blue

Factfile

Origin   Russia, pre-1800s, then redeveloped in 1965
Breed profile   Russian domestic cat + British blue
Head   Wedge shape, wide cheeks and large, pert ears
Eyes   Large, almond shape and in emerald green
Weight   7 to 12 lb.
Life span   15 to 20 years

Body
An archangel cat (its original name) is long in the body, legs and tail. Its proud, aristocratic countenance conceals a curious and energetic nature.

Fact
Blues have a unique, double-textured coat. Undercoat and guard hairs are the same length, so the blue-gray, silver-tipped coat is soft and plush.

Grooming	Weekly

British Shorthair Self

Factfile

Origin	UK, 1800s then 1950s development
Breed profile	Br. shorthair + pedigree/non-pedigree shorthairs
Head	Large head, full cheeks and sweet expression
Eyes	Large, round, wide set and usually orange
Weight	9 to 18 lb.
Life span	14 to 20 years

Body This rounded, strong cat has a broad chest with short legs on rounded paws. Its one-color coat is dense, with more fur per inch than any other breed.

Fact Most modern British shorthairs can be traced to Brynbuboo Little Monarch, a 1969 Grand Champion blue. The breed is a top-three UK pet.

Grooming	Weekly

British Shorthair Tortie

Factfile

Origin	UK, 1800s, then 1950s developments
Breed profile	Br. shorthair + pedigree/non-pedigree shorthairs
Head	Large head, full cheeks and sweet expression
Eyes	Large, round, wide set in copper, orange or gold
Weight	9 to 18 lb.
Life span	14 to 20 years

Body Torties display two colors, closely blended and in subtle patches (like a blaze on its face). A black tortie will have black and red patches.

Fact John Tenniel based his Cheshire Cat illustrations for Lewis Carroll's *Alice in Wonderland* on the British shorthair's always smiling expression.

Grooming	Weekly

40

British Shorthair Colorpoint

Factfile

Origin   UK, 1990s
Breed profile   British shorthair + Siamese
Head   Large head, full cheeks and sweet expression
Eyes   Medium to large, round, wide set and blue
Weight   9 to 18 lb.
Life span   14 to 20 years

Body   This colorpoint has the pointed coat pattern of a Siamese. Its face, ears, legs and tail are darker than its body. There are 16 colorpoint colors.

Fact   In 2011, a British shorthair was declared to have the world's loudest purr! It came in at 67.7 decibels, similar to the volume of a vacuum cleaner.

Grooming   **Weekly**

British Shorthair Bicolor

Factfile

Origin	UK, 1800s
Breed profile	British shorthair + bicolor British shorthair
Head	Large head, full cheeks and sweet expression
Eyes	Large, round, wide set in copper, orange or gold
Weight	9 to 18 lb.
Life span	14 to 20 years

Body
With its large head, thick neck, proud chest and sturdy, muscular frame, the British shorthair has been called the "bulldog of the feline world."

Fact
The bicolor comes in eight (white plus one other color) forms. Cartoon cat Sylvester was a bicolor tuxedo who looked dressed for a black-tie event.

Grooming	Weekly

Ojos Azules

Factfile

Origin	USA, 1984
Breed profile	Naturally evolved
Head	Triangular head with prominent cheekbones
Eyes	Large, round and deep blue
Weight	9 to 12 lb.
Life span	10 to 15 years (estimated)

Body The silky, fine coat on this medium-sized cat often shows white on its face, paws and the flattened tip of its tail. It is a noisy, active and affectionate breed.

Fact Ojos azules (the name is Spanish for "blue eyes") are rare – only ten were known in 1991, when the breed was recognized.

Grooming	Weekly

Egyptian Mau

Factfile

Origin	Egypt, 1950s
Breed profile	Naturally evolved
Head	Rounded, wedge shape with rounded muzzle
Eyes	Large, rounded almond shape in green
Weight	7 to 9 lb.
Life span	8 to 14 years

Body A distinct dark stripe runs along the spine of this rare, naturally spotted cat. Its forelegs are shorter than the hind, and its body is muscular and slender.

Fact Mau are fast! Long hind legs mean they can run at 30 mph. Like cheetahs, they've an extra fold of stomach skin which extends their stride.

Grooming	Weekly

Factfile

Origin	Arabian Peninsula
Breed profile	Naturally evolved from a desert wildcat
Head	Long and rounded, concave nose and large ears
Eyes	Oval, angled to the nose and most often green
Weight	9 to 16 lb.
Life span	12 to 15 years

Body Arabian mau are compact and muscly, with longer hind legs. The tabby coat comes in six colors and is fine and exceptionally glossy.

Fact Having to survive in hot deserts for over 1,000 years made them good hunters. They can jump high, are territorial, and need to explore.

Grooming	Weekly

Abyssinian

Factfile

Origin	UK, 1890s
Breed profile	Native cat + silver/brown tabbies (unconfirmed)
Head	Wedge shape with rounded crown and muzzle
Eyes	Rounded almond in amber, green or hazel
Weight	8 to 12 lb.
Life span	9 to 13 years

Body Abyssinians (or Abys) are athletic, muscular medium–large cats with slender legs. Their short coat hairs are banded (ticked), fine and close lying.

Fact Zulu was perhaps the first Abyssinian in the UK, and it was here, rather than along the Nile, in Ethiopia or Southeast Asia, that this breed was developed.

Grooming	**Weekly**

Australian Mist

Factfile

Origin	Australia, 1977
Breed profile	Burmese + Abyssinian + Australian shorthairs
Head	Broad, short wedge shape with well-spaced ears
Eyes	Large, rounded oval in shades of green
Weight	8 to 15 lb.
Life span	15 to 18 years

Body Mist have a medium–large body, broad chest, strong, slender legs and a long, thick tail. They come in six colors and lack an undercoat.

Fact Australia's first pedigreed cat has an even temperament, along with a spotted and marbled coat, with rings or bars on the tail, legs, face and neck.

Grooming   **Weekly**

Ocicat

Factfile

Origin	USA, 1964
Breed profile	Abyssinian + Siamese + American shorthair
Head	Rounded wedge shape with alert, large ears
Eyes	Large, almond shape and angled to nose
Weight	8 to 12 lb.
Life span	15 years plus

Body Most noticeable about the ocicat is its spotted smooth coat, with the clear "M" on the face. A row of spots marks the spine of this medium–large cat.

Fact Although strikingly similar to a South American jungle cat, the ocelot and ocicat share no bloodline, though the ocicat *was* bred to be an ocelot copycat!

Grooming	Weekly

Factfile

Origin	Arabuko Sokoke Rain Forest, Kenya
Breed profile	Naturally evolved
Head	Small, wedge shape, high cheeks, upright ears
Eyes	Oval, wide set and usually amber or green
Weight	6 to 10 lb.
Life span	9 to 15 years

Body Sokoke are lean, long and leggy cats with coarse fur and a whiplike tail. The coat's ticking is evident in the ground color and in the pattern.

Fact Though named for its native home, its local name is kadzonzo, meaning "looks like tree bark." This refers to the camouflage-like ring patterns on its flanks.

Grooming	Weekly

California Spangled

Factfile

Origin	USA, 1986
Breed profile	Abyssinian + Am. and Br. shorthairs + others
Head	Wedge shape, prominent cheeks, large ears
Eyes	Almond, angled to nose and amber to copper
Weight	7 to 15 lb.
Life span	10 to 15 years

Body With a low-slung walk, lean body, large paws and pale whisker pads, this tabby is like a mini leopard – and it was launched in a Neiman Marcus catalog!

Fact The plight of the leopard caused Louis Leakey to suggest breeding a leopard-like domestic cat. Only 58 spangled have been registered.

Grooming	Weekly

Toyger

Factfile

Origin	USA, 1980s
Breed profile	Striped Am. sh + Bengal + Kashmir street cat
Head	Long and broad with inverted heart muzzle
Eyes	Round with upper inside slightly hooded
Weight	7 to 15 lb.
Life span	10 to 15 years

Body This cat has a long, strong, low body and high shoulders. It is a tiger – complete with rolling gait and low-carried tail – that will go for a walk on a leash.

Fact Toygers – toy plus tiger – were bred to look like mini tigers, with branched, random vertical stripes and circular face marks on an orange coat.

Grooming	Weekly

Bengal

Factfile

Origin	USA, 1960s to 1970s
Breed profile	Asian leopard cat hybrid + domestic cat
Head	Small, rounded wedge, high cheeks, short ears
Eyes	Rounded oval, large and wide set
Weight	12 to 22 lb.
Life span	14 to 16 years

Body With long, muscular bodies, large paws, thick tails, spotted or marbled coats, and stalk-like gaits, these gentle cats are very "big cat" like.

Fact Like its wild forebears, Bengals like water and will jump in the bathtub. The domestic cat should be four generations removed from its wild ancestors.

Grooming	Weekly

Cheetoh

Factfile

Origin	USA, 2003
Breed profile	Ocicat + Bengal
Head	Broad, modified wedge shape with large ears
Eyes	Almond shape in gold, green, yellow, cold blue
Weight	8 to 23 lb.
Life span	12 to 14 years

Body Muscular and lithe, the cheetoh has the low-shouldered walk of a predator. Its thick, velvety and glossy coat is leopard spotted or rosetted.

Fact Today's lap cat is eight generations removed from its wild ancestor. It is one of the largest domestic breeds, with males dwarfing the females.

Grooming   **Weekly**

Factfile

Origin	USA, 1986
Breed profile	Serval + Siamese
Head	Small with tall forehead with large ears
Eyes	Medium in green, brown, gold with tear streaks
Weight	7 to 15 lb.
Life span	17 to 20 years

Body "Long and leggy" aptly describes this cat. Like other breeds with wild cat lineage, the hind legs are higher than its shoulders. It can be trained to fetch.

Fact A domestic version of the wild African serval, it has retained the spotted pattern, fat nose, ringed tail, tall, wide and erect ears and hooded eyes.

Grooming	Weekly

Factfile

Origin	USA, 2000
Breed profile	Bengal + Oriental shorthair
Head	Flat-topped wedge with large, high-set ears
Eyes	Large and round in gold to amber
Weight	8 to 15 lb.
Life span	8 to 12 years

Body A long neck and legs hold its muscular body in an upright posture. Its round-tipped ears should be the same length as its head.

Fact Called the "Velcro cat" because it sticks to its owners, the Serengeti will amuse itself climbing to heights and tearing around at high speed.

Grooming	Weekly

Chausie

Factfile

Origin	USA, 1990
Breed profile	Jungle cat + domestic cat
Head	Long with high cheeks, tall outward-tilted ears
Eyes	Half oval, angled upward in yellow, lime, aqua
Weight	7 to 30 lb.
Life span	12 to 14 years

Body Tall, with a long, flat-sided body, their coat's grizzled tabby pattern – alternate light and dark bands with dark hair tips – is unique to the breed.

Fact The intelligent, loyal chausie (the jungle cat's scientific name is *Felis chaus*) sometimes have the tufted ears and elongated snout of a cougar.

Grooming	Weekly

Munchkin Shorthair

Factfile

Origin	USA, 1983
Breed profile	Naturally evolved (gene mutation)
Head	Round wedge shape with obvious whisker pads
Eyes	Large, walnut shape, wide set, any color
Weight	4 to 9 lb.
Life span	12 to 14 years

Body A small–medium, short-legged cat, its body is thick and slopes upward to its rump. The semi-plush, water-resistant coat comes in many colors.

Fact Munchkin Lilieput holds the record for the shortest living cat, at only 5.25 inches. A gene mutation causes short legs in munchkins (and dachshunds).

Grooming	Weekly

Kinkalow

Factfile

Origin	USA, 1995
Breed profile	American curl + munchkin gene
Head	Tiger shaped with curled ears
Eyes	Large and round, wide set in any color
Weight	3 to 7 lb.
Life span	12 to 15 years

Body This cat's body is compact and rests on munchkin short legs. Its tail may be longer than its body, and its coat – in any color or pattern – is sleek.

Fact When born, the kinkalow has straight, upward-pointing ears. The ears begin to curl back a few months later, and are easily damaged.

Grooming	Weekly

Factfile

Origin	USA, 1990s
Breed profile	Munchkin + laPerm
Head	Broad, rounded wedge, outward pointing ears
Eyes	Medium to large walnut shape in any color
Weight	3 to 7 lb.
Life span	12 to 15 years

Body This short-legged, long-tailed cat has a coat of soft, springy curls that stand away (not lay flat) from its body. Its whiskers and eyebrows are also curly!

Fact Skookum, which means "mighty" in Chinook, aptly describes this confident, active and clever cat that may behave like a kitten forever.

Grooming	2 to 3 times a week

Lambkin Dwarf

Factfile

Origin	USA, 1987 or 1991
Breed profile	Munchkin + Selkirk rex
Head	Wedge shape with rounded ears
Eyes	Large and round in any color
Weight	5 to 9 lb.
Life span	12 to 14 years

Body Both the body and the curved, fluffy tail are long in relation to the short legs. Its coat is curly at birth, straightens at four months, and later curls again.

Fact The lambkin dwarf is rare, as only a few kittens in a litter will have the curly coat and short legs. It was named lambkin for its fleece-like coat.

Grooming 2 to 3 times a week

Bambino

Factfile

Origin	USA, 2005
Breed profile	Sphynx + munchkin
Head	Wedge shape, obvious whisker pads, huge ears
Eyes	Disproportionately large and rounded
Weight	5 to 9 lb.
Life span	12 to 15 years

Body This short-legged cat has the large upright ears, wrinkles, pink or white hairless-looking skin and sparse whiskers of a sphynx. Its skin feels like chamois leather.

Fact The bambino needs regular bathing, grooming and protection from sun and cold. Sometimes its tail tip bears a lionlike powder puff of fur.

Grooming 2 to 3 times a week

Dwelf Cat

Factfile

Origin	USA, 2000s
Breed profile	Munchkin + sphynx + American curl
Head	Long wedge shape, high cheeks, curled ears
Eyes	Large and almond shape in any color
Weight	4 to 9 lb.
Life span	12 to 15 years

Body
This stocky, "hairless," short-legged cat has a round tummy and ears that stand upright rather than curl back. Its forelegs may appear bowed.

Fact
Like other hairless breeds, the dwelf – its name is a play on "dwarf" and "elf" – may be covered in downy hair and have whiskers and eyebrows.

Grooming   2 to 3 times a week

Elf Cat

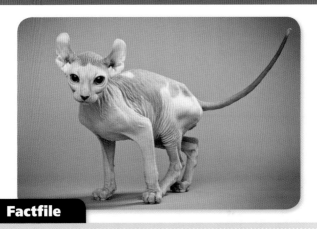

Factfile

Origin	USA, 2004
Breed profile	Sphynx + American curl
Head	Modified wedge, prominent cheeks, curled ears
Eyes	Large walnut shape, angled to nose in any color
Weight	10 to 15 lb.
Life span	12 to 15 years

Body The "hairless" elf has a muscular body and upright ears. In creating the elf, the curl genes countered the heart problem common in inbred sphynx.

Fact One of the newest hybrids and very rare, the elf, like its namesake, can be mischievous. Treasures in high places are irresistible to this agile cat.

Grooming   **2 to 3 times a week**

Ukrainian Levkoy

Factfile

Origin	Ukraine, 2004
Breed profile	Donskoy (hairless) + Scottish fold
Head	Long and angular, stepped profile, low forehead
Eyes	Long almond shape in all colors
Weight	8 to 15 lb.
Life span	12 to 15 years

Body This is a medium-sized cat with a long, "hairless" body, strong legs, inward-folding ears set high and wide, curly whiskers and a long and flexible tail.

Fact To maintain its body temperature and high metabolism, the levkoy, like all hairless breeds, has a great appetite. But this cat does *not* like heights.

Grooming	Weekly

Scottish Fold

Factfile

Origin	UK, 1961 and USA, 1970s
Breed profile	Naturally evolved + Br. and Am. shorthairs
Head	Rounded head, full cheeks, folded ears
Eyes	Large and round, wide spaced in any color
Weight	6 to 13 lb.
Life span	13 to 15 years

Body The wide-set ears point down and forward, emphasizing the face's roundness. The legs are short–medium in length, and the fur is thick and soft.

Fact It was a barn cat named Suzie whose unusual ears started the breed. To solve genetic issues, folds in the US were bred with shorthairs.

Grooming	Weekly

Foldex

Factfile

Origin	Canada, 1992
Breed profile	Scottish fold + exotic shorthair
Head	Rounded head, short muzzle, folded ears
Eyes	Wide and round in any color
Weight	6 to 14 lb.
Life span	12 to 15 years

Body At 21 days old, the ears of this medium-size rounded cat drop forward along a crease, like the fold's. With multiple creases, the ears will lie completely flat.

Fact Behind its appealing teddy bear look, some foldex carry a fold gene problem. To avoid this, a straight-ear cat should be bred with a folded-ear cat.

Grooming — **Weekly**

Highlander Shorthair

Factfile

Origin	USA, 2004
Breed profile	Desert lynx + jungle curl
Head	Inverted pear shape, long forehead, curled ears
Eyes	Large and wide set in any color
Weight	10 to 20 lb.
Life span	10 to 15 years

Body While they have the lynx muscular, large body and bobbed tail, their upright and loosely backward curled ears are their main feature.

Fact The Highlander is a regal cat that likes to clown around. Being kept active is important, and they need plenty of human and feline company.

Grooming	Weekly

67

Factfile

Origin	USA, 1981
Breed profile	Naturally evolved (gene mutation)
Head	Modified wedge with straight nose, curled ears
Eyes	Large, wide set and walnut shape in any color
Weight	5 to 10 lb.
Life span	12 to 15 years

Body This long, muscular cat has large ears that curve backward. The curl develops four days after birth, and is fully formed and hard about four months later.

Fact The original curl was Shulamith, a street stray of no specific pedigree. Because of this, the breed is robust, healthy and of even temperament.

Grooming	Weekly

Japanese Bobtail Shorthair

Factfile

Origin	Japan, 1600s or possibly China and Korea
Breed profile	Naturally evolved
Head	Broad and curved triangle shape, wide-set ears
Eyes	Oval in any color but often blue or gold
Weight	5 to 10 lb.
Life span	9 to 15 years

Body This slender, long-legged (its longer hind legs make it a great jumper!) cat has a two- to three-inch bobbed tail that looks like a furry pom-pom.

Fact The bobtail is the paw-waving *Maneki-neko* good-luck cat. Though many are calico, this cat's tangle-free coat comes in all colors and patterns.

Grooming	Weekly

Kurilean Bobtail Shorthair

Factfile

Origin	Kuril Islands, Russia, 1990
Breed profile	Naturally evolved
Head	Large, rounded wedge, erect, forward tilt ears
Eyes	Large, rounded, angled to nose, yellow to green
Weight	7 to 15 lb.
Life span	12 to 20 years

Body A compact, muscular body ends with a bobbed, bent, spiraled or curved tail, two to five inches long. The hind legs are longer than the forelegs.

Fact Though found in harsh, cold climates, this bobtail has a dense coat with little undercoat. It is a proficient hunter on land and in water, and a good climber.

Grooming	Weekly

70

Mekong Bobtail

Factfile

Origin	Southeast Asia, Iraq and Iran
Breed profile	Naturally evolved
Head	Rounded wedge shape with large, wide ears
Eyes	Large, almond shape in an intense blue
Weight	8 to 10 lb.
Life span	15 to 18 years

Body A medium-sized sturdy body sits on slender legs – the hind being longer than the fore – and oval paws. Its tail is short and kinked or curved.

Fact The Mekong bobtail's coat is close lying, glossy with a crisp texture, and pointed like the Siamese. It is an active cat that likes to climb and jump.

Grooming   **Weekly**

American Bobtail Shorthair

Factfile

Origin	USA, 1960s
Breed profile	Naturally evolved
Head	Broad, wedge shape with strong brow and pads
Eyes	Almond in deep sockets and in any color
Weight	7 to 16 lb.
Life span	13 to 15 years

Body A wild look – shaggy fur over a long body on round paws, short tail and alert, tufted ears – belies a sociable temperament and gentleness.

Fact There is absolutely no wild bobcat heritage in this entertaining family pet. The only thing it is likely to stalk and leave on the doormat is a cuddly cat toy!

Grooming	Weekly

Factfile

Origin	Isle of Man, UK, pre-1700s
Breed profile	Naturally evolved
Head	Rounded with full cheeks and wide-set ears
Eyes	Large and round in copper, green, hazel or blue
Weight	8 to 12 lb.
Life span	8 to 14 years

Body The Manx is medium sized, and unlike similar types, kicks its long, strong hind legs to accelerate rapidly. Its back is arched; its chest, broad.

Fact There are up to five recognized tail lengths for this cat, from rumpy (tailless) and rumpy riser, to stumpy, stubby and longy (short tailed).

Grooming	Weekly

Pixiebob Shorthair

Factfile

Origin	USA, 1987
Breed profile	Naturally evolved
Head	Inverted pear emphasized by fluffy facial hair
Eyes	Triangular, deep set in gold, brown, green
Weight	8 to 18 lb.
Life span	12 to 14 years

Body A muscular, heavy-boned cat with broad chest (sometimes topped with a neck ruff) and long hind legs, it can be tailless or bobtailed.

Fact Pixiebobs can have up to seven toes on each foot (polydactylism). They are bred to resemble the North American bobcat, but there is no shared bloodline.

Grooming	Weekly

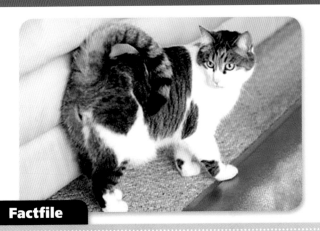

Factfile

Origin	USA, 1998
Breed profile	Cat with curled tail + Ragdoll + Am. shorthair
Head	Broad, wedge shape, medium-sized ears
Eyes	Large, almond shape in any color
Weight	7 to 14 lb.
Life span	15 to 20 years

Body Ringtails are long and muscular, with a strong, flexible back, long forelegs and long, webbed toes that spread to aid climbing.

Fact A stray named Solomon started this unique breed that curls its tail over its back when relaxed. Its vertebrae are not fused, so it can also hold its tail straight.

Grooming	Weekly

75

Sphynx

Factfile

Origin	Canada and USA, 1966 to 1978
Breed profile	Hairless domestic cat + Devon rex
Head shape	Wedge shape with obvious cheeks and muzzle
Eyes	Large, lemon shape, angled and in any color
Weight	6 to 11 lb.
Life span	12 to 20 years

Body A coat of downy hair covers this muscular cat's barrel-chested body. Its tail is whiplike; its face, unique. Like similar cats, the sphynx seeks warmth.

Fact The sphynx – named for a human-headed, lion-bodied mythical creature – has chamois-like skin that shows the colors that its fur would have been.

Grooming	2 to 3 times a week

Donskoy

Factfile

Origin	Russia, 1987
Breed profile	Naturally evolved (gene mutation)
Head	Wedge shape with tall, large upright ears
Eyes	Small almond shape, angled up, in any color
Weight	6 to 12 lb.
Life span	12 to 15 years

Body Donskoy's long, muscular, wrinkled body sits on strong legs with long webbed toes. The tail is thin and tapers to a point, and the ears are wide set.

Fact There are four types of donskoy: rubber (bald), flocked (chamois-like), velour (hair on extremities) and brush (some bald spots).

Grooming   **2 to 3 times a week**

Peterbald

Factfile

Origin	Russia, 1994
Breed profile	Donskoy + Oriental and Siamese shorthairs
Head	Triangular with long muzzle, wide-set large ears
Eyes	Large, almond shape, angled and in any color
Weight	6 to 12 lb.
Life span	10 to 15 years

Body This slim bodied and elegant cat has bat-like flared ears, a thin tail and wrinkled skin. It has a laser-like stare and is intelligent and affectionate.

Fact Peterbalds have oval paws and webbed toes which can grasp objects, such as lever door handles. Like the donskoy, coat types and colors vary.

Grooming 2 to 3 times a week

LaPerm Shorthair

Factfile

Origin	USA, 1982
Breed profile	Naturally evolved (gene mutation)
Head	Modified wedge shape, long neck, upright ears
Eyes	Medium–large almond shape and in any color
Weight	5 to 10 lb.
Life span	10 to 15 years

Body LaPerms are moderate in every way – there are no extremes in body type or traits, and working-cat ancestry means they are robust, clever and resourceful.

Fact The Shirley Temple-like ringlets and curls are tightest on the belly, throat and ear bases. The longest hairs circle the neck, and the soft coat may have a parting.

Grooming	2 to 3 times a week

Selkirk Rex Shorthair

Factfile

Origin	USA, 1987
Breed profile	Plush-haired domestic cat + Persian
Head	Rounded and broad with padded whisker pads
Eyes	Large, round eyes in all colors
Weight	9 to 16 lb.
Life span	10 to 15 years

Body This cat's dense, soft coat – tousled and messy or coiffured – in all colors and markings, conceals a medium-sized sturdy body and gentle nature.

Fact Birth curls straighten at eight months and redevelop over the next two years. This is the only breed named for a person – the breeder's stepfather.

Grooming 2 to 3 times a week

80

Cornish Rex

Factfile

Origin	Cornwall, UK, 1950s
Breed profile	Wavy-coated domestic cat + Siamese
Head	Egg shape, high cheeks, large upright ears
Eyes	Large and oval, wide set and in any color
Weight	5 to 10 lb.
Life span	11 to 15 years

Body The "greyhound of cats" has an athletic body, arched back and long, thin tail and legs (notably hind legs). It is famed for its crimped, low-lying coat.

Fact While most cats have three layers to their coats, this rex only has an undercoat. It sheds hair, can get bald patches and was endangered in the 1960s.

Grooming **Weekly**

Devon Rex

Factfile

Origin	Devon, UK, 1959
Breed profile	Curly-coated feral cat + domestic cat
Head	Small on a long neck, upturned nose, large ears
Eyes	Large, oval and wide set
Weight	6 to 9 lb.
Life span	9 to 15 years

Body Though similar to a Cornish, the Devon's face is wider, its ears more flared and its body shorter and heavier. The wavy coat has the full three layers.

Fact Much of the Devon's appealing "alien" look comes from its extra-large, upright, low-on-the-face ears and oversized eyes.

Grooming   **Weekly**

German Rex

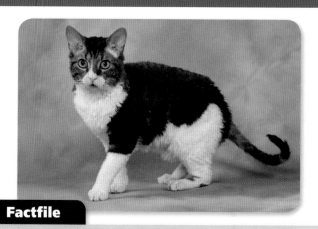

Factfile

Origin	Germany, 1951 to 1957
Breed profile	Naturally evolved (gene mutation)
Head	Round with obvious cheeks, forward tilt ears
Eyes	Rounded in blue, green gold, and hazel
Weight	5 to 8 lb.
Life span	9 to 14 years

Body This cat is medium sized but stands tall on its slender legs. The first German rex was named "little lamb" because of its short, fluffy, curly coat.

Fact Cornish and German rex are similar genetically, but despite a breeding program and export to other countries, the German rex is very rare.

Grooming	Weekly

American Wirehair

Factfile

Origin	USA, 1966
Breed profile	Naturally evolved (gene mutation)
Head	Round, high cheekbones and prominent muzzle
Eyes	Large, round and usually golden or odd eyed
Weight	8 to 15 lb.
Life span	7 to 12 years

Body This wirehair is medium sized but powerful, like an American shorthair. Its coat is likened to a terrier's – springy, crimped, and wiry to the touch.

Fact The coat needs almost no grooming, except in spring when old growth sheds. The gene which creates the coat has only ever appeared in the US.

Grooming	Weekly

Aphrodite Giant

Factfile

Origin	Cyprus, 1st century CE
Breed profile	Naturally evolved
Head	Triangular with strong chin, medium to large ears
Eyes	Oval or almond in pale yellow, blue and green
Weight	11 to 24 lb.
Life span	12 to 15 years

Body A strong, big-boned cat, it has a long body, hind legs longer than the fore and a woolly soft coat that comes in all types save pointed and mink.

Fact The Aphrodite is one of two Cyprus breeds that were shipped to Cyprus to ravage the snake population. The cats were isolated for 1,200 years.

Grooming 2 to 3 times a week

Factfile

Origin	Cycladic Islands, Greece
Breed profile	Naturally evolved
Head	Broad triangle shape with round-tipped ears
Eyes	Almond shape in greens, blues, and yellows
Weight	9 to 10 lb.
Life span	9 to 12 years

Body This bi- or tricolor cat is muscular, lean and athletic, and very healthy. Its island environment means it will hunt in water. Its coat is semi-long.

Fact Possibly one of the oldest domesticated breeds, formal breeding of this unique native cat only started in the 1990s. It is a Greek national treasure.

Grooming	Weekly

Lykoi

Factfile

Origin	USA, 2010
Breed profile	Naturally evolved (gene mutation)
Head shape	Wedge shape with tall, wide-based pointed ears
Eyes	Large, round and yellow
Weight	5 to 13 lb.
Life span	12 to 15 years

Body A lithe, solid body sits on long legs. Facial features are hairless – its nose is leathery – and legs and feet are sparsely haired. It sheds a lot, almost to bald.

Fact A solid-color birth coat changes to solid, tip-to-root white or black hairs. The very sparse coat and lean profile earned it the nickname, "werewolf cat."

Grooming	2 to 3 times a week

Factfile

Origin	Russia, 1988
Breed profile	Bob-tailed Siamese + short-tailed Siamese
Head	Wedge shape, rounded snout and erect ears
Eyes	Large and oval in blue, gold green, blue green
Weight	2 to 6 lb.
Life span	16 to 22 years

Body Though it is small, its body is surprisingly muscly and robust. Its bobbed tail measures one to two inches. Its legs and body are in perfect proportion.

Fact Even when mature, this cat is no bigger than a kitten aged three to six months. It was not bred to be a mini version of a breed; it is naturally diminutive.

Grooming	Weekly

Persian Self

Factfile

Origin	UK, 1871 (first shown)
Breed profile	Ancient breed
Head	Large with round face, full cheeks, short muzzle
Eyes	Large and round in copper, green or blue
Weight	8 to 15 lb.
Life span	12 to 16 years

Body This cat is adored for its long, fine-textured coat, full ruff and snubbed nose cradled between large eyes. Its legs are short, but its tail is luxurious.

Fact Modern Persian cats have minimal links to the early cat from Persia (Iran). With seven self colors, it is one of the most popular breeds in the US.

Grooming	Daily

Persian Chinchilla

Factfile

Origin	UK, 1894 (first shown)
Breed profile	Blue Persian + silver tabby (unconfirmed)
Head	Large with round face, full cheeks, short muzzle
Eyes	Large and round in green or blue green
Weight	4 to 7 lb. (smaller than other Persians)
Life span	12 to 16 years

Body The white or golden undercoat has black or blue tips; facial features are also outlined in black or blue. Nose and paw pads can be red, black or blue.

Fact The chinchilla is named for the similarly colored South American rodent. It's a comedown for the glamour-puss of the feline world.

Grooming   **Daily**

Persian Smoke

Factfile

Origin	UK, 1880s
Breed profile	Black/blue Persians + silver tabby (unconfirmed)
Head	Large with round face, full cheeks, short muzzle
Eyes	Large and round in copper
Weight	8 to 15 lb.
Life span	12 to 16 years

Body Each of this cat's hairs is pale at the base, growing gradually darker toward the tip. Its coat can be black, blue, cream, red or tortoiseshell.

Fact The Persian cat's coat stands away from the body, and the hairs can be four inches long. Like all longhairs, Persians shed – a lot – multiple times a year.

Grooming	Daily

Persian Bicolor

Factfile

Origin	UK, 1800s (unconfirmed)
Breed profile	Ancient breed
Head	Large with round face, full cheeks, short muzzle
Eyes	Large and round in copper, green or blue
Weight	8 to 15 lb.
Life span	12 to 16 years

Body Bicolor cats have a patterned coat of white plus one or two other colors (calico coat) including black, red, blue, cream, chocolate or lilac.

Fact Pre-1955, bicolors were not accepted in US cat shows, and many newborns were rejected. Attitudes and rules then changed, making them fashionable.

Grooming	Daily

Persian Tabby

Factfile

Origin	UK, 1800s (unconfirmed)
Breed profile	Ancient breed
Head	Large with round face, full cheeks, short muzzle
Eyes	Large and round in copper or green and hazel
Weight	8 to 15 lb.
Life span	12 to 16 years

Body There are two types of Persian face: doll-face cats have pointed features, while pekes have ultra-flat faces that can result in breathing problems.

Fact Daily grooming and regular bathing are necessary, but this breed adores the attention. The Persian is not very active, so is prone to obesity.

Grooming	Daily

Himalayan

Factfile

Origin	USA and UK, 1920s to 1950s
Breed profile	Persian + Siamese
Head	Large with round face, full cheeks, short muzzle
Eyes	Large and round in blue
Weight	7 to 14 lb.
Life span	9 to 15 years

Body The "Himmy" has a Persian's short, thick body and legs, flat face and coat, but with Siamese color points. The points begin to show at around 16 weeks.

Fact Some cat associations give this cat breed status, while others class it as a variety of Persian. As with Persians, they can have doll or peke faces.

Grooming	Daily

Balinese

Factfile

Origin	USA, 1950s
Breed profile	Naturally evolved (gene mutation)
Head	Wedge shape with large, wide-based ears
Eyes	Almond shape, angled to nose and in vivid blue
Weight	6 to 11 lb.
Life span	18 to 22 years

Body Balinese have the long, slender body and legs of the Siamese. The tail is long and full, and the coat comes in many point colors and patterns.

Fact This cat is not named for the island of Bali (Siamese came from Thailand), but for the grace and poise that reminded an early breeder of Balinese dancers.

Grooming	Weekly

Burmilla Longhair

Factfile

Origin	UK, 1981
Breed profile	Chinchilla Persian + lilac Burmese
Head	Rounded with wide cheeks, forward tilt ears
Eyes	Almond shape and usually green
Weight	10 to 13 lb.
Life span	10 to 15 years

Body A medium-sized cat with rounded chest, straight back, slender legs (hind legs longer than fore) and oval paws. Its tipped, silky fur is thick and dense.

Fact Distinctive features of the burmilla are its sparkling silver base coat, "M" mark on the forehead and black or brown outlined nose, lips and eyes.

Grooming — **Weekly**

York Chocolate

Factfile

Origin	USA, 1983
Breed profile	Black longhair + black-and-white longhair
Head	Rounded wedge with a medium to long muzzle
Eyes	Rounded almond shape in green, hazel or gold
Weight	10 to 16 lb.
Life span	13 to 15 years

Body This cat's large, solid body is wrapped in light, soft, glossy chocolate-colored fur that resists matting. The fur is thickest on chest, neck and breeches.

Fact The York was bred using domestic and farm cats chosen on the basis of coat color. This active and vocal outdoor cat was named for New York.

Grooming	**Weekly**

Oriental Longhair

Factfile

Origin	UK, 1950s
Breed profile	Siamese + Russ. blue/Br. sh/Abyssinian/domestic
Head	Wedge shape with large, wide-based ears
Eyes	Almond shape in green, blue or odd eyed
Weight	6 to 12 lb.
Life span	13 to 15 years

Body This longhair has a long, slender and tubular body, neck and limbs. Its tail is plumed. Orientals come in over 300 different colors and patterns.

Fact Also known as the Mandarin, this is an active and clever cat. A great climber and jumper, it has been known to open refrigerator doors!

Grooming   2 to 3 times a week

Tiffanie

Factfile

Origin	UK, 1981
Breed profile	Naturally evolved (gene mutation)
Head	Short wedge shape with wide-set medium ears
Eyes	Large and wide set in yellow to green
Weight	8 to 14 lb.
Life span	12 to 18 years

Body A medium-sized, muscular cat with a dense, soft and silky coat that lies flat on the spine and feathers on the tummy. Its long tail is plumed.

Fact Tiffanies came from the mutation that causes long hair in the burmilla. Its coat is tangle free, so grooming is easier than might be expected.

Grooming	**2 to 3 times a week**

Chantilly–Tiffany

Factfile

Origin	USA, 1969
Breed profile	Semi-foreign longhair + semi-foreign longhair
Head	Broad, wedge shape with round-tipped ears
Eyes	Oval, angled to nose, deep yellow to rich amber
Weight	7 to 14 lb.
Life span	14 to 16 years

Body
This medium-sized cat is known for its silky lush coat, usually but not always chocolate colored, and plumed tail. Its tufted ears point forward and outward.

Fact
It was once thought that Burmese longhairs were used in breeding, but this has been disproved. Chantilly-Tiffany are registered under both names.

Grooming 2 to 3 times a week

Birman

Factfile

Origin	Myanmar or perhaps France, 1919
Breed profile	Siamese + Angora or Persian (unconfirmed)
Head	Broad and rounded with medium-sized ears
Eyes	Round and sapphire blue
Weight	6 to 12 lb.
Life span	12 to 16 years

Body The Birman is a stocky, powerful cat clothed in a silky coat of Siamese point colors. The fur on its tummy is wavy, and its neck has a ruff.

Fact One legend of this sacred temple cat is that in thanks for its devotion to a priest, a goddess gave it a golden coat, blue eyes and pure-white paws (gloves).

Grooming	2 to 3 times a week

Maine Coon

Factfile

Origin	USA, 1800s
Breed profile	Imported longhairs + domestic shorthairs
Head	Wedge shape, high cheeks and wide-set ears
Eyes	Round in gold, copper, green or odd eyed
Weight	11 to 25 lb.
Life span	10 to 15 years

Body This is a big, strong and handsome cat that can be 40 inches long! Its thick, shaggy and glossy coat would have protected it during freezing Maine winters.

Fact Brought to the US as mousers on ships, longhairs mated with domestic cats, and their progeny became farm cats. Maine coon are regarded as native cats.

Grooming	Daily

Ragdoll

Factfile

Origin	USA, 1960s
Breed profile	Domestic longhair + Birman and (later) Persian
Head	Broad wedge shape, round muzzle, wide-set ears
Eyes	Large, oval and blue
Weight	10 to 20 lb.
Life span	12 to 17 years

Body Ragdolls are large and heavily boned. The colorpoint, bicolor or mitted coat is silky and forms a ruff on the neck and breeches on the legs.

Fact This very calm cat is totally at ease being handled, flopping like a rag doll. But it is a myth that it doesn't feel pain, and it is *not* an alien hybrid.

Grooming	**2 to 3 times a week**

Ragamuffin

Factfile

Origin	USA, 1994
Breed profile	Ragdoll + Persian/Himalayan/domestic longhair
Head	Broad rounded wedge, flared forward tilt ears
Eyes	Large and in amber, blue, gold, green and hazel
Weight	8 to 20 lb.
Life span	12 to 16 years

Body Ragamuffins' rectangular bodies are fronted by broad chests with wide shoulders and hind ends. The fur gets longer from head to tail.

Fact The aim of this cat's breeding program was to improve its genetic health by widening the gene stock. Point colors were bred out in this process.

Grooming	2 to 3 times a week

Somali Longhair

Factfile

Origin	USA, 1960s to 1970s
Breed profile	Abyssinian + longhair Abyssinian
Head	Triangular shape with small contour, large ears
Eyes	Dark rimmed, almond shape in green and gold
Weight	8 to 12 lb.
Life span	12 to 15 years

Body Muscular, lithe and graceful, the Somali's arched back and alert nature give the impression it is about to pounce. Its tail tapers to a full brush.

Fact In its red, ruddy or sorrel form, it's been given names like miniature lion and fox cat. Each fine hair in its coat can display 4 to 20 color bands.

Grooming	2 to 3 times a week

British Longhair

Factfile

Origin	UK, 1910s and 1940s
Breed profile	British shorthair + Persian + Russian blue
Head	Round and full with small, broad-based ears
Eyes	Large and round in gold to copper, blue or green
Weight	9 to 18 lb.
Life span	18 to 20 years

Body Like its shorthair relative, this longhair has a sturdy build, full chest, strong legs and chubby face with "chipmunk" cheeks. Its coat is dense and luxurious.

Fact The coat begins to thicken in the autumn, in preparation for winter. Grooming must then be increased to avoid tangles and matting.

Grooming	2 to 3 times a week

Nebelung

Factfile

Origin	USA, 1986
Breed profile	Naturally evolved
Head	Modified wedge with large, wide-set ears
Eyes	Slightly oval, wide set in yellow to green
Weight	7 to 15 lb.
Life span	11 to 16 years

Body Nebelungs are long, sturdy and muscly. The dense and soft coat makes them appear rounder, with tail hair longer than body hair.

Fact Two Russian blue-type cats but with semi-long coats started the nebelung line. The name means "mist" and refers to its floating blue to gray coat.

Grooming   **2 to 3 times a week**

Norwegian Forest Cat

Factfile

Origin	Norway, 1950s
Breed profile	Naturally evolved
Head	Triangular shape with tufted high-set ears
Eyes	Almond, angled to nose and in any color
Weight	7 to 20 lb.
Life span	14 to 16 years

Body Often likened to the Maine coon, it is big, sturdy and imposing. The long coat is glossy, while extra-strong claws make for an excellent climber.

Fact Perhaps traveling to Norway with the Vikings 1,000 years ago, its woolly undercoat and water-shedding top coat developed to tolerate cold.

Grooming	2 to 3 times a week

Turkish Van

Factfile

Origin	Lake Van, Turkey
Breed profile	Naturally evolved
Head	Broad, wedge shape with round-tipped ears
Eyes	Large, oval, pink rimmed and in blue or amber
Weight	10 to 20 lb.
Life span	12 to 17 years

Body The Turkish van is a sturdy and muscular colored cat with white patches; color should appear on its head, tail and over 15 percent of its body.

Fact An ancient cat, it is rare in its native home and is protected. As a water lover with a water-repellent coat, it's known as the "swimming cat."

Grooming	2 to 3 times a week

Turkish Vankedisi

Factfile

Origin	Eastern Turkey, pre-1700
Breed profile	Naturally evolved
Head	Broad, wedge shape with round-tipped ears
Eyes	Large oval, pink rimmed in blue and/or amber
Weight	10 to 20 lb.
Life span	12 to 17 years

Body This is a pure-white version of the Turkish van with a full-brush tail. Odd-eyed – one blue, one amber – cats are the most highly regarded.

Fact Vankedisi, like many all-white cats, have a genetic tendency to deafness. They are rare and revered, so few have been exported from Turkey.

Grooming   2 to 3 times a week

Turkish Angora

Factfile

Origin	Ankara region, Turkey
Breed profile	Naturally evolved
Head	Modified wedge with large, tufted ears
Eyes	Walnut shape in blue, green, amber and yellow
Weight	6 to 12 lb.
Life span	12 to 18 years

Body Angoras have a long, sinuous body on long legs with tufts on the toes. It can be odd eyed, and its silky, soft coat is wavy on the tummy.

Fact A national treasure, this cat was used in the breeding program for the Persian's coat. Best known is the white Angora, but it comes in many colors.

Grooming	2 to 3 times a week

Siberian

Cats

Longhair

Factfile

Origin	Russia
Breed profile	Naturally evolved
Head	Short, broad wedge with rounded contours
Eyes	Large and round in gold to green, some blue
Weight	10 to 20 lb.
Life span	11 to 18 years

Body The Siberian is powerfully built, and its muscular hind legs make it an excellent jumper. Its glossy, textured coat is dense and water-repellent.

Fact Formal breeding of this native cat did not start until the 1980s, and its numbers are low outside of Russia. It may be hypoallergenic.

Grooming	Daily

112

Neva Masquerade

Factfile

Origin	Neva River, Russia, 1970s
Breed origin	Siberian + Balinese, Siamese and Himalayan
Head	Broad head, full cheeks and medium-sized ears
Eyes	Large, slightly oval and deep blue (preferred)
Weight	11 to 22 lb.
Life span	10 to 18 years

Body The Neva is Siberian, from its muscular build to its long coat, bushy tail and tufted ears and toes. Its dense, low-lying undercoat is snug and warm.

Fact This colorpoint variation of a Siberian wears a "mask" of darker fur across the top of its face. It is the only forest cat breed allowed colorpoint.

Grooming	2 to 3 times a week

Munchkin Longhair

Factfile

Origin	USA, 1980s
Breed profile	Munchkin + domestic longhair
Head	Modified wedge shape, high cheeks, alert ears
Eyes	Walnut shape, well spaced and in any color
Weight	5 to 9 lb.
Life span	12 to 14 years

Body This cat – a twin of its shorthaired and short-legged relative – has a semi-long all-weather coat, including a ruff. Its tail is plumed; its breeches, shaggy.

Fact With its low center of gravity, the munchkin will surprise with its speed and cornering ability. It can jump, especially onto a lap, but prefers life on the ground.

Grooming	2 to 3 times a week

Napoleon

Factfile

Origin	USA, 1995
Breed profile	Munchkin + Persian, exotic sh and Himalayan
Head	Round and domed, long nose and round cheeks
Eyes	Round and wide and in all colors and odd eyed
Weight	5 to 9 lb.
Life span	12 to 15 years

Body Rounded from its tufted ears and huge ruff to its plumed, fluffy tail, this short-legged cat is strong and muscly. It is small in size, but big in character.

Fact Also known as the minuet, this rare cat blends Persian beauty with munchkin build, perhaps named for the diminutive but dynamic Emperor Napoleon.

Grooming	Daily

Scottish Fold Longhair

Factfile

Origin   Scotland
Breed profile   Scottish fold + British longhair
Head   Round head, firm jaw and forward-folded ears
Eyes   Large and round in all colors but often copper
Weight   6 to 13 lb.
Life span   13 to 15 years

Body
This is a rounded, mid-sized cat with a long, soft coat – in all colors and patterns – that stands away from the body. The tail is plumed; the neck ruffed.

Fact
In a normal litter, half the kittens will have the folded ears, the rest upright (the cat's hearing is not affected). It is also known as a Highland fold.

| Grooming | 2 to 3 times a week |

American Curl Longhair

Factfile

Origin	USA, 1981
Breed profile	Naturally evolved (gene mutation)
Head	Modified wedge with straight nose, curled ears
Eyes	Large, walnut shape, wide set in any color
Weight	5 to 10 lb.
Life span	12 to 15 years

Body Instantly recognizable by ears that curl back at least 90 degrees, the longhair's semi-long coat lays flat and is silky and fine.

Fact American curls are affectionate, smart and curious, and refuse to grow up – a "Peter Pan" cat. They are indoor cats and still relatively uncommon.

Grooming	Weekly

Highlander Longhair

Factfile

Origin   USA, 2004
Breed profile   Desert lynx (hybrid) + jungle curl (hybrid)
Head   Inverted, pear shape, long forehead, curled ears
Eyes   Large and wide set in any color
Weight   10 to 20 lb.
Life span   10 to 15 years

Body
The curled-eared Highlander has a thick 2.5-inch-long coat that is almost shaggy in places. Its fluffy tail does not extend beyond the hocks.

Fact
This big cat can be born with extra toes, so it might grasp objects and open doors. Its ears curl vertically (a curl's fold horizontally) and stand tall.

Grooming   2 to 3 times weekly

Japanese Bobtail Longhair

Factfile

Origin	Japan, 1600s or possibly China and Korea
Breed profile	Naturally evolved
Head	Broad and curved triangle with wide-set ears
Eyes	Oval in any color but often blue or gold
Weight	5 to 10 lb.
Life span	9 to 15 years

Body This cat's medium-sized, long, slender body is covered with a silky, long coat that forms "pantaloons" on the hind legs. It has minimal undercoat.

Fact Legend has it that long ago a cat's tail caught fire. It ran through the town leaving fires in its wake, so the emperor ordered all tails bobbed.

Grooming	2 to 3 times a week

Kurilean Bobtail Longhair

Factfile

Origin	Kuril Islands, Russia, 1990
Breed profile	Naturally evolved
Head	Large, rounded wedge and forward tilt ears
Eyes	Large, rounded and angled in yellow to green
Weight	7 to 15 lb.
Life span	12 to 20 years

Body The coat is silky, and is longer on the neck, stomach and thighs. The bobtail can have one or more kinks, be "S" shaped or spiraled.

Fact Not all cats with long hair need grooming multiple times a week. Where the undercoat is minimal, weekly is enough until molting.

Grooming	Weekly

Pixiebob Longhair

Factfile

Origin	USA, 1987
Breed profile	Naturally evolved
Head	Inverted pear emphasized by fluffy facial hair
Eyes	Triangular, deep set in golden brown or green
Weight	8 to 18 lb.
Life span	12 to 14 years

Body Hairs in this longhair's soft coat are two inches in length and lie close to the body. The fur on the face is bushy and grows downward.

Fact For a cat whose backstory includes the legend of wild cat ancestors, it behaves like a dog. It follows its owners and will go for walks on a leash.

Grooming   **Weekly**

American Bobtail Longhair

Longhair

Factfile

Origin	USA, 1960s
Breed profile	Naturally evolved (gene mutation)
Head	Broad, wedge shape with strong brow and pads
Eyes	Almond in deep sockets and in any color
Weight	7 to 16 lb.
Life span	13 to 15 years

Body This bobtail's one-to-four-inch tail is flexible. It can be straight, curved or kinked, or have bumps along its length. It uses its tail to communicate.

Fact These bobtails are rare and expensive – breeders can charge $1,000! Some truck drivers own bobtails – company on long haul trips.

Grooming	2 to 3 times a week

Cymric

Factfile

Origin	Isle of Man and Canada, 1960s
Breed profile	Naturally evolved
Head	Round head, prominent cheeks, large ears
Eyes	Large and round, slightly angled in any color
Weight	7 to 13 lb.
Life span	8 to 14 years

Body This muscular cat has a broad chest and long hind legs. It has a double coat, with longer fur on the neck and upper legs. It can be tailless or tailed.

Fact Some class the Cymric as a separate breed, others as a longhair Manx. Until formal breeding in the 1960s, longhaired kittens were regarded as mutants.

Grooming	**2 to 3 times a week**

Selkirk Rex Longhair

Factfile

Origin	USA, 1987
Breed profile	Plush-haired domestic + Persian
Head	Rounded and broad with padded whisker pads
Eyes	Large and round in all colors
Weight	9 to 16 lb.
Life span	10 to 15 years

Body This rex has the "woolly sheep" look in abundance. Its fur is softer than shorthair fur, and long ruff hairs frame the face. Its tail curls form a plume.

Fact A Selkirk litter might have kittens with curly, straight, long and short coats, but all will be alert and active with sweet, even temperaments.

Grooming	**2 to 3 times a week**

LaPerm Longhair

Factfile

Origin	USA, 1982
Breed profile	Naturally evolved (gene mutation)
Head	Modified wedge shape, long neck, upright ears
Eyes	Medium to large almond shape and in any color
Weight	5 to 10 lb.
Life span	10 to 15 years ears

Body LaPerms have long, curly, Daliesque whiskers and very soft coats of curls and ringlets, along with long, crimped eyebrows that may need trimming.

Fact LaPerms are not as difficult to groom as most people think. They have very little undercoat to shed, so regular brushing keeps the curls in good order.

Grooming	Weekly

Glossary

Almond shape Eyes that are oval with one end tapered and the other rounded.

Bicolor A white coat with patches of one solid color.

Blue A blue-gray coloration.

Bobtail A short or absent tail due to a gene mutation.

Breeches Long fur on the upper half of hind legs above hocks.

Breed Cats with a similar, defined appearance and related ancestry.

Breed standard Ideal characteristics for a breed.

Calico White coat with spots or patches of two other colors, often orange and black.

Classic tabby Swirls on flanks, "butterfly" on shoulders, stripes on legs and "M" on forehead. Also called blotched or marbled.

Close- or low-lying Fur that lies flat and smooth against the body.

Colorpoint Darker colored fur on face, ears, tail and paws.

Crossbreed Mating two different breeds. Offspring are hybrids.

Domestic A cat (often house cat) of unknown or mixed breed.

Feline Member of the cat family, including big and small cats.

Feral A domestic cat that has reverted to a wild state.

Formal breeding Planned program of cross- or outbreeding to develop or improve a natural or pedigree breed.

Gene DNA unit of information for specific features.

Guard hairs Top layer of the coat and often long and coarse.

Hypoallergenic Unlikely to cause an allergic reaction.

Kinked A malformation, especially of the tail.

Lilac Pale, pinkish-gray color.

Litter A group of kittens born to one female cat at the same time.

Longhair Fur is longer than on a shorthair, the tail often plumed and the neck encircled by a ruff.

Louis Leakey A pioneer in the study of human evolution and wildlife conservation.

Mackerel tabby Vertical stripes – continuous or broken – on flanks and stomach, lines across face and "M" on forehead.

Mask Darker fur on the face that resembles an eye mask.

Mitted White points on paws, chin and chest.

Mutation A change in a gene to produce an unexpected alteration.

Muzzle Part of a cat's face containing the nose and jaws..

Naturally evolved Often an ancient or native breed that has developed without interference.

Odd eyed One eye in one color, the other in a second color.

Pointed (*See Colorpoint*)

Plume Soft hairs that grow on the end of a cat's tail.

Polydactylism Extra toes that are produced by a genetic mutation.

Rex A curly or wavy coated breed.

Ruff Long hair on neck and chest.

Rumpy A tailless cat.

Seal Dark-brown coloring.

Self All coat hairs in one color.

Shaded The final quarter of each hair is colored.

Shorthair Smooth, sleek coat of short hairs.

Smoke Hair tips are dark colored, middle section is lighter in color and the base even paler or white.

Stumpy A cat with a residual tail.

Tabby A mackerel, classic, spotted or ticked coat pattern.

Temperament A cat's personality.

Tipped A coat pattern where just the tip of each hair is colored.

Tortoiseshell Black and red hairs are mixed in patches over the coat.

Tufts Clusters of long hairs, which are often seen between the toes or on the ears.

Undercoat Beneath the top coat and usually short, thick and plush.

Wedge shape Straight lines from outer ear bases to jaw. Modified wedge is not as extreme.

Whiskers The long, stiff hairs growing on the face of a cat.

Index

Abyssinian 46
Aegean 86
American bobtail
  longhair 122
  shorthair 72
American Burmese 18
American curl
  longhair 117
  shorthair 68
American ringtail 75
American shorthair 34
American wirehair 84
Aphrodite giant 85
Arabian mau 45
Asian
  shaded Burmilla 12
  smoke 13
  tabby 14
Australian mist 47
Balinese 95
bambino 61
Bengal 52
Birman 101
Bombay 15
Brazilian shorthair 36
British
  longhair 106
British shorthair
  bicolor 42
  colorpoint 41
  self 39
  tortie 40
burmilla longhair 96
California spangled 50
Chantilly-Tiffany 100
chartreux 37
chausie 56
cheetoh 53
Chinese li hua 11
Cornish rex 81
Cymric 123
Devon rex 82
donskoy 77

dwelf cat 62
Egyptian mau 44
elf cat 63
European Burmese 17
European shorthair 35
Exotic shorthair 8
foldex 66
German rex 83
Havana brown 27
Highlander
  longhair 118
  shorthair 67
Himalayan 94
Japanese bobtail
  longhair 119
  shorthair 69
khao manee 9
kinkalow 58
korat 10
kurilian bobtail
  longhair 120
  shorthair 70
lambkin dwarf 60
laPerm
  longhair 125
  shorthair 79
lykoi 87
Maine coon 102
Manx 73
Mekong bobtail 71
munchkin
  longhair 114
  shorthair 57
Napoleon 115
nebelung 107
Neva masquerade 113
Norwegian forest cat
  108
ocicat 48
ojos azules 43
Oriental longhair 98
Oriental shorthair
  bicolor 26
  foreign white 20
  self 21
  shaded 23
  smoke 22

  tabby 24
  tortie 25
Persian
  bicolor 92
  chinchilla 90
  self 89
  smoke 91
  tabby 93
peterbald 78
pixiebob
  longhair 121
  shorthair 74
ragamuffin 104
Ragdoll 103
Russian blue 38
Savannah 54
Scottish fold
  longhair 116
  shorthair 65
Selkirk rex
  longhair 124
  shorthair 80
Serengeti 55
Seychellois 32
Siamese
  self pointed 29
  tabby pointed 30
  tortie pointed 31
Siberian 112
singapura 16
skookum 59
snowshoe 33
sokoke 49
Somali longhair 105
sphynx 76
Thai 28
tiffanie 99
Tonkinese 19
toybob 88
toyger 51
Turkish Angora 111
Turkish van 109
Turkish vankedisi 110
Ukrainian levkoy 64
York chocolate 97